THE LEGACY OF THE ANCIENT WORLD

AFRICA AND ASIA

MACDONALD YOUNG BOOKS

First published in 1995 by Macdonald Young Books
Campus 400
Maylands Avenue
Hemel Hempstead
Hertfordshire HP2 7EZ
Originally published in 1994 as part of the title *Pathways,
Timelines of the Ancient World.*

A CIP catalogue for this book is available from the
British Library

ISBN 0 7500 1810 0

Commissioning Editor: Thomas Keegan
Editors: Jill A. Laidlaw, Samantha Armstrong
Designer: Simon Borrough
Picture Researcher: Juliet Duff
Illustrators: Swanston Publishing Ltd., Jonathan Potter,
Robina Green, Steve Roberts,
Deborah Kindred (Simon Girling & Associates)
Adrian Barclay, Lee Montgomery (Beehive Illustration)

Text copyright © 1994 Mike Corbishley
Illustrations copyright © 1994 Macdonald Young Books

Printed in Portugal

Cover illustration: **Swanston Publishing Ltd: right**. **Robina
Green**: left.

Cover photograph: Robert Harding Picture Library

Map artwork: Swanston Publishing Ltd.

Picture Acknowledgements
The author and publisher would like to acknowledge, with
thanks, the following photographic sources:

Ancient Art & Architecture Collection: 25. **C. M. Dixon**: 11.
Robert Harding: cover, 13 left, 13 right.

CONTENTS

Words in **bold** are explained in the glossary on
pages 26–7.

INTRODUCTION

Today it is possible to travel thousands of kilometres by air from one continent to another in just a few hours. The world seems like a small place because images of people from far-off countries are beamed into our front rooms on to our television sets. In ancient times, travel was difficult and slow — many parts of the world would have been far too dangerous for strangers. Even today, people without modern technology, such as jet travel and television, often know little about the lands and the peoples beyond their own countries, or even beyond their own villages.

Despite these difficulties, there were connections between ancient peoples thousands of years ago. *The Legacy of the Ancient World* tells the stories of some of those connections. This book talks about some of the most important peoples of India, Africa and Asia and finds out about some of the legacies they have left to us today.

INDIA AND AFRICA

Part 1 shows you the Indus Valley Civilization and the impressive stone walls of Great Zimbabwe. Travel across the road that connected three continents — the Silk Road — the world's longest trade route, linking China and beyond to western Europe.

CHINA

Some of the world's most complex and wealthy societies developed in China. During some periods of China's history, communication with other parts of the world was banned. At other times the Chinese looked abroad for trade and made voyages of exploration themselves.

Throughout *The Legacy of the Ancient World* you will find Time Lines (below). The key dates and events listed in the Time Lines will help you to see what is happening in each civilization. You will be able to relate these dates to some of the things happening in other places all over the world.

THE INDUS VALLEY CIVILIZATION

BC

c. 3500 First farming villages in the Indus Valley

c. 2500 Indus Valley Civilization established
Cities of Mohenjo-daro and Harappa built

THE WORLD

BC

c. 8500 First rock art in the Sahara region
First cultivation of wild grasses in Peru

c. 8300 Glaciers retreat in Europe

c. 7000 First crops cultivated in Mexico and in New Guinea

c. 6500 Britain separates from Europe

Dates are given in the usual way — BC and AD. AD is an abbreviation of two **Latin** words *Anno Domini*. Latin was the language used by the Romans. These two words mean "in the year of the lord". This was the system of dating invented by the Christians. Dates are counted from the birth of Jesus Christ. This system of dating is used in most parts of the world today. For example, the first astronauts to step on to the surface of the moon did so on in July AD 1969 — but this date is usually just written as 1969. Dates before the birth of Christ are counted backwards and have the letters BC after them. For example, the Roman general, Julius Caesar, first invaded Britain in 55 BC and then in the following year, 54 BC.

Sometimes we do not know precise dates for something that happened a very long time ago. You will see the letter c. used before dates like these. It is also an abbreviation of a Latin word, *circa*, which means 'about'.

CITY PLANNING

Farming people began to settle in the Indus Valley around 3500 BC. Mohenjo-daro was the largest city of the Indus Valley Civilization. The city was carefully built to a plan and houses were connected to the city's sewage and waste disposal systems.
See pages 10–11.

SEAL STONES

We know that there was a great deal of contact between the cities of the Indus Valley and other places, such as the Persian Gulf, because of trade. Merchants used carved stones to put a seal on bales (bundles) of goods such as cotton and spices.
See page 11.

A STONE CITY

Great Zimbabwe is the largest ancient building of Black Africa. The city reached the height of its power around AD 1350. Huge stone structures were built there, including some walls ten metres high. Zimbabwe (the name of the modern country) comes from the **Shona** language dzimba dza mabwe meaning 'houses of stone'.
See page 17.

JENNE-JENO

The remains of Africa's oldest city, Jenne-jeno, can be found in the modern state of Mali. Some of the houses of Jenne-jeno were built in a traditional round style but others were square or rectangular. African houses are usually circular so these rectangular houses show the influence of African trade with the peoples of the **Near East**.
See page 16.

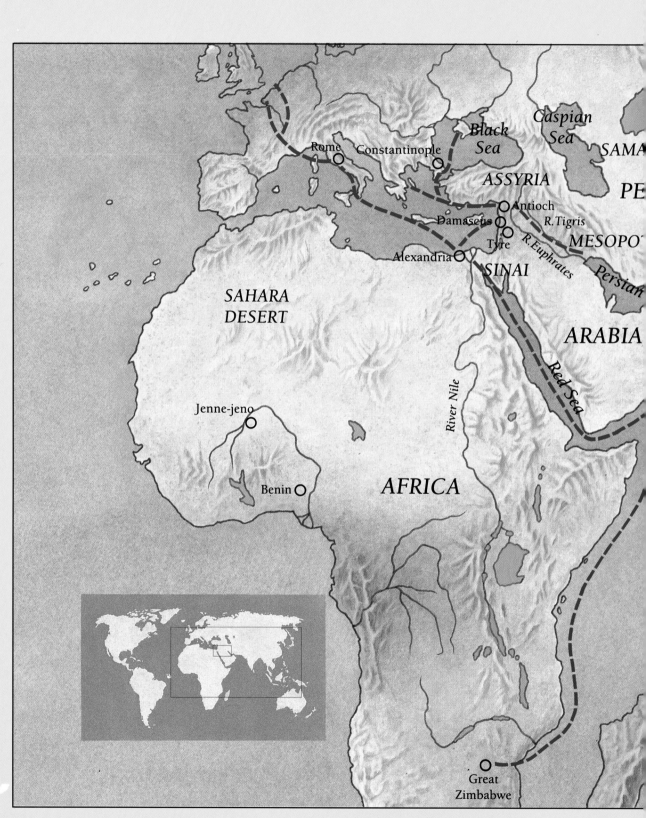

RICH KINGDOMS

The kingdoms of west Africa were very wealthy. They traded north across the Sahara Desert and south-west within the continent itself. Thousands of beautiful objects were made out of gold, brass and ivory.
See page 16.

MYSTERIOUS SILK

Chinese silk has always been an expensive and sought-after cloth. It was **exported** from China to as far away as Britain. People in the West could not understand how it was made.
See pages 14–15.

AFRICAN EXPORTS

Many of the peoples of Africa exported goods to Arabia, China and India. Arab sailors and merchants settled along the east coast of Africa and set up trading stations. The Arabs acted as middlemen — this means that they bought goods off African merchants and sold them on to foreign traders who visited the busy ports of the African coastline.

HOUSES WITHOUT WINDOWS

There were no windows in the outside walls of houses in Indus Valley towns — only the door opens on to the street. There were windows inside the house facing into a central courtyard. When it was very hot people slept outside on the flat roofs — just as people do today in hot countries. See page 10.

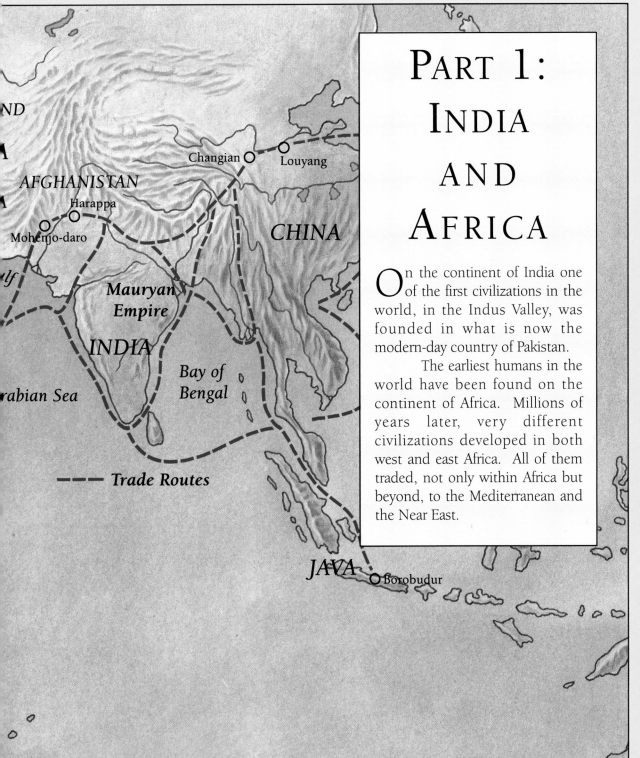

EMPERORS AND VICEROYS

The emperors of the Mauryan Empire governed their lands through viceroys who each toured their own province to make sure that everything was in order. The emperor even sent his own inspectors to make sure his viceroys were doing their jobs. The people, who were mostly farmers, paid taxes to the emperor.
See page 12.

PART 1: INDIA AND AFRICA

On the continent of India one of the first civilizations in the world, in the Indus Valley, was founded in what is now the modern-day country of Pakistan.

The earliest humans in the world have been found on the continent of Africa. Millions of years later, very different civilizations developed in both west and east Africa. All of them traded, not only within Africa but beyond, to the Mediterranean and the Near East.

BUDDHISM

It was during the time of the Mauryan Empire of India that the religion of Buddhism was really established, although the Buddha himself, Siddhartha Gautama, had been born around 566 BC. The first Buddhist monuments and monasteries were built during the reign of Emperor Asoka. See page 13.

SELLING SILKS AND SPICES

*A series of **caravan** routes stretched from China to the Mediterranean carrying silk and many other luxury goods such as pottery, metalwork, ivory and spices. Goods were also carried to the West by sea, around India and to Europe via the Red Sea and the Persian Gulf. See pages 14–15.*

BUDDHIST MONKS

*Buddhist monks lived in communities in monasteries. The most important part of each monastery was the stupa. It was here that the **sacred** objects of the religion were kept and **rituals** held. The stupa was originally a simple earth mound. Over time it changed into a mound-shaped stone building.*
See page 13.

THE INDUS VALLEY CIVILIZATION

The Indus Valley Civilization of ancient India is named after the River Indus, in the modern-day country of Pakistan. A number of large cities were built along the Indus River around 2500 BC. An **archaeologist**, called R. D. Banerjii, discovered the city of Mohenjo-daro (below) in 1922. The cities of this earliest Indian civilization were carefully planned and contained hundreds of houses, shops, public buildings and workshops. The cities were defended by surrounding brick walls. The first farmers settled in this area around 3500 BC. It was an area full of wildlife and the land was rich and suitable for growing crops because the rainfall was higher than it is now. The people of the Indus Valley grew wheat, barley, vegetables and, in some places, rice. They kept animals such as cattle, sheep, pigs, dogs and buffaloes. They probably used horses, elephants and camels for farming, trade and travel. Around 1900 BC the climate altered and over the next few hundred years floods destroyed good farming land and mud clogged up the coastline. Places which had once been busy harbour cities found themselves inland. The cities fell into disrepair and people moved to small farms.

BC
c. 3500 Llama first used as a pack
animal in Peru
First city civilizations
established in Sumeria
c. 3000 Coastal regions of
Australasia occupied by
hunters and fishers
First evidence of Egyptian
hieroglyphic writing

THEIR ACHIEVEMENTS

The people of the Indus Valley built the world's first sewage system. Under the regularly laid-out streets, brick drains carried waste from houses and workshops out of town. The drains could be checked at regular intervals through inspection chambers at street level. The streets were also probably guarded by police — little buildings like sentry boxes have been found at street corners.

c. 2300 Settlements in Mesoamerica
c. 2000 First settlers in New Guinea
Inuits (Eskimos) reach
northern part of Greenland
c. 1450 Eruption on island of Thera
End of Minoan civilization

MOHENJO-DARO

This city covered an area of about 60 **hectares** and had a population of about 40,000 people. The buildings were constructed from mud-bricks baked in the sun — the bricks were exactly the same size in all of the Indus Valley cities.

HARAPPA

Further to the north-east on one of the **tributaries** of the River Indus was the other main Indus Valley city, Harappa. This city was similar to Mohenjo-daro but smaller with a population of about 25,000 people.

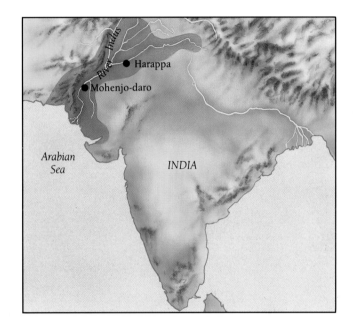

CITIES

On the left is a drawing of the city of Mohenjo-daro. In the centre of the city there was a huge raised mound with public buildings on it — a great bath-house which was probably used in religious rituals, a wooden grain store 45 metres long, an assembly hall and a temple. The people of Mohenjo-daro lived in the lower town. Most people lived in one-room apartments. The rich lived in large two-storeyed houses (above). Rooms were grouped around an open courtyard. Some houses had their own water supply and lavatories. Houses were connected to a sewage system and had rubbish disposal points on their outside walls.

TRADE

The cities were major centres of trade. Each city had a huge number of workshops making pottery and metal tools, jewellery and cloth. We know there was trade between the Indus Valley, the Persian Gulf and **Mesopotamia**. There were also overland trade routes to Persia and Afghanistan. There was a standard system of weights and measures. Bales of goods for shipment were marked with seals like the one below. The writing is **hieroglyphic** but it has not been **deciphered** — perhaps it records the name of the merchant or company shipping the goods.

This **bust** of a bearded man (below) was found in Mohenjo-daro. He was probably a priest or a king.

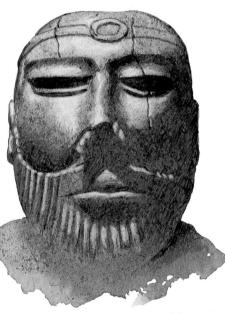

THE MAURYAN EMPIRE

Sometime around 1500 BC people, called Aryans, arrived in north-west India. They dominated the people who were there before them and built large cities. Gradually they spread east and settled on the land of the upper Ganges. By 600 BC there were at least 16 small states in the plain of the River Ganges. In the next century these states were constantly at war with each other. The strongest state took control of the others and eventually they were all taken over by the Kingdom of Magadha. At the end of the fourth century BC the kingdom was seized by Chandragupta Maurya. He was the first real emperor of India and his territory, the Mauryan Empire (left), stretched over most of the continent of India.

Chandragupta's grandson, Emperor Asoka, came to power in 269 BC and made the empire even bigger. He kept very close control of his lands. The people, most of whom were farmers, paid taxes to him. These taxes paid for things like the road system, the **civil servants** who organized the state and Asoka's huge conquering army.

TRADE

There was trade throughout the different states of the Mauryan Empire and with other countries. The Romans **imported** many goods from India at this time, including ivory, cotton cloth, spices (below) and precious stones. Roman writers tell us about trade with India and there were even Roman trading stations on the southern coasts of the continent. The Roman writer **Pliny** wrote that it was '*40 days voyage from the Red Sea to the first trading station in India, which was called Muziris*'.

FARMING

The people of the Mauryan Empire were farmers but the land they farmed was actually owned by the emperor. People paid taxes on the land they farmed, the crops they produced and the animals they reared. The emperor could order land to be cleared for agriculture and moved people by force from one place to another if the population became too large. **Irrigation** was essential if the land was to be farmed properly. Rivers were **dammed** and **reservoirs** created. Canals took water to irrigate terraces like these on the right. When irrigation schemes were provided by the state, the farmers had to pay an extra water tax.

BC

c. 1500 Mycenaean civilization established

c. 1000 Phoenician alphabet introduced

Kingdom of Israel ruled by King David

c. 900 Chavín civilization in the Andes, south America

THEIR LEGACIES

*The Mauryan Empire was responsible for two very important events. One affected the boundaries of the **subcontinent** of India — for the first time in this part of the world huge numbers of people were controlled and governed as one country. After Emperor Asoka's death his great empire began to break up. The other significant event of this period — Buddhism — is still with us today. The Buddhist religion spread to many eastern countries. Today there are over 500 million followers of Buddhism.*

509 Last Etruscan king, Tarquinius Superbus, Tarquin the Proud, expelled by the Romans

c. 400 Celts migrate into northern Italy

334 Alexander the Great begins his campaigns against the Persians

250 All of Italy is controlled by the Romans

BUDDHISM

One of the world's greatest religions, Buddhism, was founded in India during the time of the Mauryan Empire. Siddhartha Gautama was born around 566 BC into a rich family. At the age of 29 he saw four signs which changed his life. He decided to leave home and search for what he called the True Wisdom. After six years he reached *Nirvana*, or **enlightenment**, and became the 'Buddha' which can be translated as the 'Enlightened One'. For the next 45 years he preached a very simple philosophy — that Nirvana could be reached by doing good works and **meditating**. After his death a group of followers established an order of Buddhist monks to spread Siddhartha's beliefs. Buddhism spread beyond the Mauryan Empire to South East Asia, China and Japan.

A statue of Buddha in India (top) and modern-day Buddhist monks in India (above).

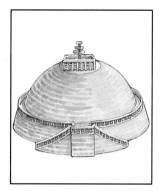

The Great Stupa at Sanchi, in India.

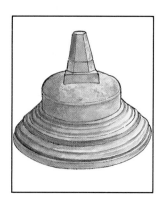

The stupa at Borobodur, in Java.

A stupa at Sarnath, in India.

MONASTERIES AND STUPAS

The Emperor Asoka converted to Buddhism and it became the main religion of his empire. The emperor helped spread the religion by ordering Buddhist **inscriptions** to be carved on to flat rock surfaces and specially-made pillars. He also helped build monasteries for Buddhist monks. In the centre of each monastery was a special building called a stupa (left and below) for the rituals of the religion. The first stupas were simple mounds of earth but later were made into round stone buildings. Temples were built to cover the small stupas which often contained holy **relics**. As Buddhism spread stupa buildings became more elaborate and were often decorated with statues and carvings.

THE SILK ROAD

BC
c. 550   First silks appear in the West, in Greece
c. 100   Silk Road fully open from China to the West

AD
c. 250   Sassanians control much of the trade in spices
618–   Tang Dynasty in China
907   Silk Road traffic increases

THE SILK ROAD

651   Muslims control the silk and spice routes
1405   Silk Road trade in decline China explores sea routes for spice trade
1450   Chinese Ming rulers cut links with the outside world
1514   Portuguese ships arrive in China for the first time

The most important trade route in Asia and Europe was called the Silk Road. It stretched from China to the waters of the Mediterranean. We know that Chinese silk had reached Greece by 550 BC. But it was not just silk that was traded along this route. Many other luxury goods were carried as well, including fine pottery and spices. The Silk Road was not actually a road at all but a series of caravan routes between towns and desert **oases**. Goods were also transported by sea from the Far East, around India and through the Persian Gulf or the Red Sea.

ITALY
Rome •
GREECE
Mediterranean Sea
Black Sea
Ephesus •
TURKEY
Caspian Sea
Tyre •
IRAQ
IRAN
Arabian Sea
IND

GLASSWARE
The **Sogdian** people, who lived in the Samarkand region of central Asia, were merchants in the middle of the Silk Road. They traded goods brought from the Far East but also made objects. They made these glass vessels in the eighth century AD.

THE WORLD

BC
508   Democratic government established in Athens
c. 200 Nazca civilization at its height
30   Egypt made a Roman province

AD
29   Jesus Christ crucified
100   Paper first used in China
330   New capital of Roman Empire founded at Constantinople

THEIR LEGACIES

The Silk Road helped far-off lands to communicate. Ideas as well as goods were carried from the Far East and from the West. People in the Roman Empire wanted to buy exotic eastern goods. Cooking in western Europe was influenced and changed by the introduction of new Far-eastern spices. Several peoples still trade in the goods their ancestors sold along the Silk Road hundreds of years ago.

450   Teotihuacán becomes the sixth-largest city in the world
1096   First western Christian Crusade to the Holy Land
1347   Black Death begins to sweep through Europe
c. 1350 Maori people in New Zealand build fortified settlements
1492   Christopher Columbus reaches the Bahamas

CERAMICS

Today we use the word china for fine pottery objects, such as plates and cups. This plate (above) with a blue and white pattern was copied from ancient Chinese designs. It was made in Worcester in England in the nineteenth century.

METALWORK

Many finely-made metal objects were exported from China. This drinking cup (above) was made during the **Tang Dynasty** (in about AD 730). Its decoration shows that the Chinese artist was influenced by designs introduced from the **Sassanian Empire**.

SILK

The Chinese discovered how to make the finest cloth in the world from silkworms. The two pieces above were made in China around the eighth century AD. At first only Chinese silk reached the West. Then other people, like the Sogdians, wove silk cloth from Chinese threads. In the sixth century AD, the Persians brought silkworms from China to the **Byzantine** court.

 Xi'an

HIMALAYA

CHINA

Pacific Ocean

SPICES

Exotic flavourings extracted from plants were carried to western Europe from as near as Arabia and as far away as the islands of the Pacific Ocean. Spices like nutmeg (above) were used in cooking, perfumes, cosmetics and medicine.

15

AD
c. 100   Kingdom of Axum
         established in Ethiopia
c. 400   First towns built south of
         the Sahara Desert
c. 450   Iron-working by the Nok
         people of west Africa
c. 500   Arrival of Bantu people
c. 700   Kingdom of Ghana
         Arabs begin trading with
         African cities south of the
         Sahara Desert
c. 750   Jenne-jeno's city wall is
         completed

AFRICA

c. 1000 West African trading towns
         flourish
1054   Muslim conquest of west
         Africa begins
c. 1200 Kingdoms of Benin and
         Mali established
1324   King of Mali visits Cairo,
         Egypt
c. 1350 Great Zimbabwe at its height
         Kingdom of Songhai
         established.
         A university is established at
         Timbuktu
1450   Great Zimbabwe in decline

The earliest ancestors of human beings came from Africa millions of years ago. There were wealthy and advanced civilizations in Africa centuries before any Europeans set foot on the continent. In the north, the Egyptian civilization influenced and traded with other peoples in the Mediterranean and within Africa. Further south, along the Red Sea, the Kingdom of Axum (see coin right) played an important part in trade with Rome and with the **Kushan Empire** in India. In west Africa a number of civilizations flourished and traded iron and gold north across the Sahara Desert and to the south-east. The kingdoms of east Africa built large cities and ports and traded with the **Muslims**, the Indians and the Chinese.

BENIN

Benin was an important kingdom in what is now southern Nigeria. It thrived in the eleventh and twelfth centuries and its capital city was called Benin. The king, who was also the religious leader, was called the *oba*. He lived with his courtiers in a great palace in the walled city of Benin. The people of Benin traded pepper, **palm oil**, ivory and slaves.

JENNE-JENO

From about AD 400 the people of Jenne-jeno were trading iron and gold north across the Sahara Desert, and food with neighbouring peoples. There were around 1,000 houses inside its walls by about AD 1000.

IVORY

This highly-decorated ivory bracelet (above) is the work of a skilled **Edo** carver from Benin.

BRONZE

This bronze head (above) was cast by a **Yoruba** metalworker in the eighth century AD.

IGBO UKWU

On the left is a drawing of a burial of an important person found at Igbo Ukwu. He was probably a ruler or a priest of a small kingdom from the eighth to ninth centuries AD. He was buried sitting on a stool surrounded by expensive objects in a decorated wooden chamber. Five other people, thought to be slaves, were buried on top of his chamber — perhaps as sacrifices to accompany their master on his journey to the next life. The people of Igbo Ukwu exported ivory and food in exchange for copper from the Sahara Desert. They must also have traded with places much further away as beads imported from India have been found at this site.

THEIR LEGACIES

*The vast continent of Africa produced very different cultures and civilizations — from Egypt, to Benin, to Great Zimbabwe. The kingdoms of east and west Africa traded throughout the rest of the known world. But some Arab and European countries began to **exploit** the peoples of Africa and took large numbers of them away as slaves. Nineteenth-century white **immigrants** who came across the ruins of Great Zimbabwe did not believe that they had been built by Black Africans.*

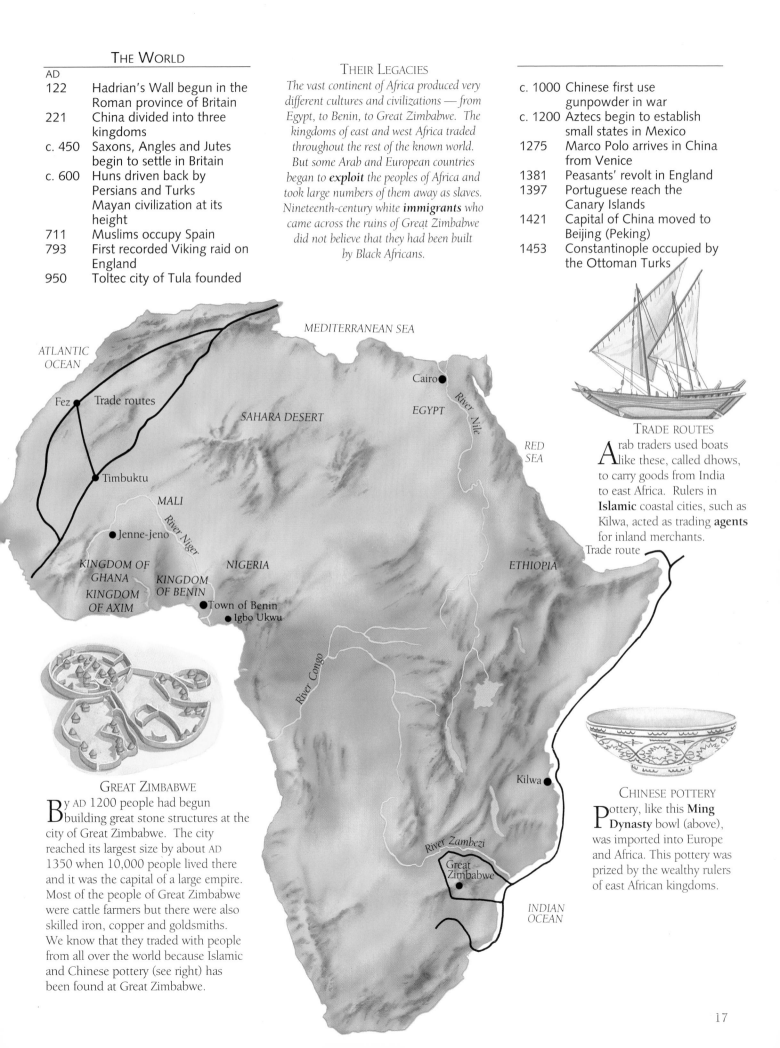

TRADE ROUTES

Arab traders used boats like these, called dhows, to carry goods from India to east Africa. Rulers in **Islamic** coastal cities, such as Kilwa, acted as trading **agents** for inland merchants.

GREAT ZIMBABWE

By AD 1200 people had begun building great stone structures at the city of Great Zimbabwe. The city reached its largest size by about AD 1350 when 10,000 people lived there and it was the capital of a large empire. Most of the people of Great Zimbabwe were cattle farmers but there were also skilled iron, copper and goldsmiths. We know that they traded with people from all over the world because Islamic and Chinese pottery (see right) has been found at Great Zimbabwe.

CHINESE POTTERY

Pottery, like this **Ming Dynasty** bowl (above), was imported into Europe and Africa. This pottery was prized by the wealthy rulers of east African kingdoms.

17

WOOD AND EARTH
Buildings of the Shang period were made by ramming dry earth between wooden shuttering. In the king's palace at the first Shang capital of Erlitou, timbers held up the overhanging thatched roofs and the strong entrance gateways.
See page 21.

PICTURES, WRITING AND ART
Like other ancient writing, the first Chinese writing was in the form of pictographs (called characters). This writing became very complex and thousands of characters were used — most of which are still in use today. The Chinese also invented calligraphy — beautiful writing considered to be an art form. Artists used brushes and ink to draw both pictures and words.
See page 20.

CLAY WARRIORS
The most incredible tomb excavated from ancient China is that of the First Emperor, Ch'in. Pits around his burial place contained thousands of full-size warriors made from pottery. Each one must have been modelled on a real person as they are all different. In earlier times in China real soldiers would have been sacrificed when the king died.
See pages 24–5.

JADE AND GOLD CLOTHES
Rich and important people of the Han Dynasty were buried in a number of different ways. Underground tombs contained their preserved bodies and possessions. The bodies of Prince Liu Sheng and his wife, Tou Wan, were encased in suits made of thousands of pieces of **jade** carefully sewn together with gold wire.

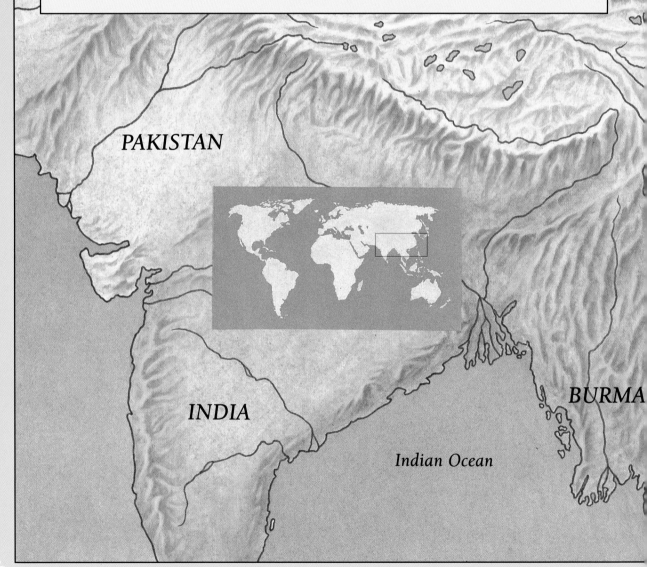

PART 2: CHINA

The first real civilization in China began around 1600 BC with the Shang Dynasty. For many years there was little contact between the people of China and the West. By the third century BC the many little kingdoms of China were unified into one large country and contact with the outside world was made through trade. The Chinese invented their own writing and measuring systems and laws. They built large cities and could grow enough food to support huge populations.

PAKISTAN

INDIA

Indian Ocean

BURMA

THE ART OF LACQUER
Han artists were famous for the beautiful objects they made. One type of art, called lacquerwork, was made only in the Far East. Wooden objects such as bowls, cups and trays, were coated with a transparent (see-through) **lacquer**. The lacquer gives a shine to the object and brings out the colours. See page 24.

THE SILK TRADE
During the Han Dynasty trade with the West became very important. The Silk Road (see pages 14–15) became a busy route. In the West, and especially in the **Roman Empire**, Chinese silk fetched high prices. In exchange, the Chinese wanted luxury goods such as furs, precious stones and ivory.

JADE AND METAL
Before metal was discovered, the Chinese used stone to make tools like axe heads. The stone had to be chipped into shape and then sanded smooth. Some axes were made from jade, which the Chinese liked to use for carving even after they had discovered bronze and iron.

BRONZE ANIMALS
Artists made very elaborate and beautiful objects from bronze during the Shang Dynasty. Bronze, a mixture of copper and tin, had to be heated in furnaces and poured into clay moulds. Animals were often featured on bronze objects and always had a significance.
See page 21.

ANYANG
Anyang was the final capital city of the Shang Dynasty. The capital had been in two other cities before. A wall ran right round the city to protect it and the houses and streets were laid out carefully inside. Outside the walls there were burial grounds and places for industries such as pottery making and metalworking.

MONGOLIA

THE GREAT WALL

○ Anyang
○ Erlitou

Yellow Sea

CHINA

JAPAN

Pacific Ocean

.... **Han Empire**
– – – **Shang Empire**

TAIWAN

South China Sea

THAILAND

THE EMPEROR'S NAME
China got its name from Emperor Ch'in Shih Huang-ti. After centuries of fighting between small states and kingdoms, he emerged as the strongest leader. He ruthlessly forced other princes to obey him and united a vast area of land into one country.
See pages 22–3.

A HUGE WALL
*Perhaps the greatest building project ever undertaken was the Great Wall of China begun in 214 BC by Emperor Ch'in. He ordered a stone wall to be built across China's northern frontier to keep out the **nomadic** tribes. Watchtowers provided extra security and were also used as signalling points to raise the alarm in time of war.*
See page 22–3.

SHANG CITIES
At the height of its power the Shang Empire was made up of over 1,000 walled cities. All of these cities were connected in some way with the capital, Anyang.

BC
1766   According to legend the first Shang king, T'ang, overthrows the Hsia Dynasty
c. 1600   Real beginning of the Shang Dynasty
c. 1400   Capital moves from Zhengzhou to Anyang

THE SHANG DYNASTY

1400   12 kings rule from Anyang for 273 years
c. 1350   Oracle bone inscriptions
1027   Last Shang king, Chou Hsin, overthrown by the Chou people. Chou Dynasty begins

Civilizations in China developed on the **fertile** lands in the valleys of the Wei and Yellow rivers in northern China. Ruling families, called dynasties, controlled large areas of land. The people of the Shang Dynasty (1600–1027 BC) believed that their kings were descended from the supreme god, Shang Ti, who founded the world. The king was in control of everything and had a large army to back him up which was paid for from taxes collected from the people. Kings and queens were buried with large numbers of precious objects as well as sacrificed people and animals.

DAILY LIFE

Most people of the Shang Dynasty were farmers. The Shang kings were in charge of great irrigation schemes which allowed the fields to produce more crops. The main food crops were rice and **millet** but wheat was also grown. Farmers also kept animals such as cattle, sheep, horses, goats, pigs, chickens and dogs. Dogs were often sacrificed along with humans for the burials of Shang rulers. While most people lived in small farming settlements, there were also large towns and cities. Cowrie shells were imported from the Pacific and Indian oceans and were considered so precious that they were used as money.

This **ritual** vessel (left) was found in the tomb of a Shang king. It would have been filled with sweet-smelling wine as a gift to the king's ancestors.

WRITING

Chinese writing developed around 1500 BC. It was based on pictographs. But in China writing developed quite differently from the way it became used in other parts of the world. Each character showed both the sound of the word and its meaning. From around 1400 BC the Chinese engraved characters on oracle bones. These were animal bones or tortoiseshells on which questions were engraved. Questions were asked about important future events, a person's health or even the weather. The bones were heated in a fire and the cracks were interpreted as answers about the future. More and more characters were developed — by AD 100 there were about 9,000.

Characters were painted with a brush and ink on to paper, or engraved on bone or metal. These characters spell out the name Fu Hao. She was a member of the royal family and was buried at Anyang (see opposite).

BC
- c. 1800 Assyrians invade northern Babylonia
- c. 1550 New Kingdom of Egypt established
- c. 1500 Aryan peoples invade northern India

THEIR LEGACIES

The Shang Dynasty gave China its first real civilization. Many beautiful cities and palaces were built. Even in the twentieth century new Chinese buildings are being built which are based on the plan of a typical Shang palace. Bronze was first worked during this period and many of the shapes and designs first made by Shang metalworkers were copied by much later Chinese peoples.

- c. 1450 Eruption on Thera, end of Minoan civilization on Crete
- 1339 Pharaoh Tutankhamun buried
- c. 1200 Hittite Empire collapses
- c. 1000 People reach almost every island in Polynesia

ERLITOU

The earliest capital of the Shang Dynasty was at Erlitou. This is what the palace of the king is thought to have looked like (above). Like other royal palaces, it consists of wooden buildings on a raised earth platform.

A RICH WOMAN'S TOMB

This is the tomb of Fu Hao, the wife of a Shang king. Above her wooden coffin, hidden in its burial chamber, were the sacrificed bodies of 16 people and six dogs. One thousand-six hundred objects, mostly made of bronze, were also buried with her.

SHANG METALWORK

The Shang Dynasty is famous for its fine bronze metalwork. Good supplies of copper and tin could be mined near the capital cities. Most objects were made by pouring molten (liquid) bronze into moulds made of fired clay. Many objects were highly-decorated and very complicated to make. The Chinese believed that animals were able to communicate with their ancestors in the spirit world. Many objects, like this one on the left, have animals on them. The tiger is protecting the man and the vessel was used for pouring out liquids during religious or burial ceremonies. The vessel on the right is called a *ting* and was also used for preparing food during religious ceremonies.

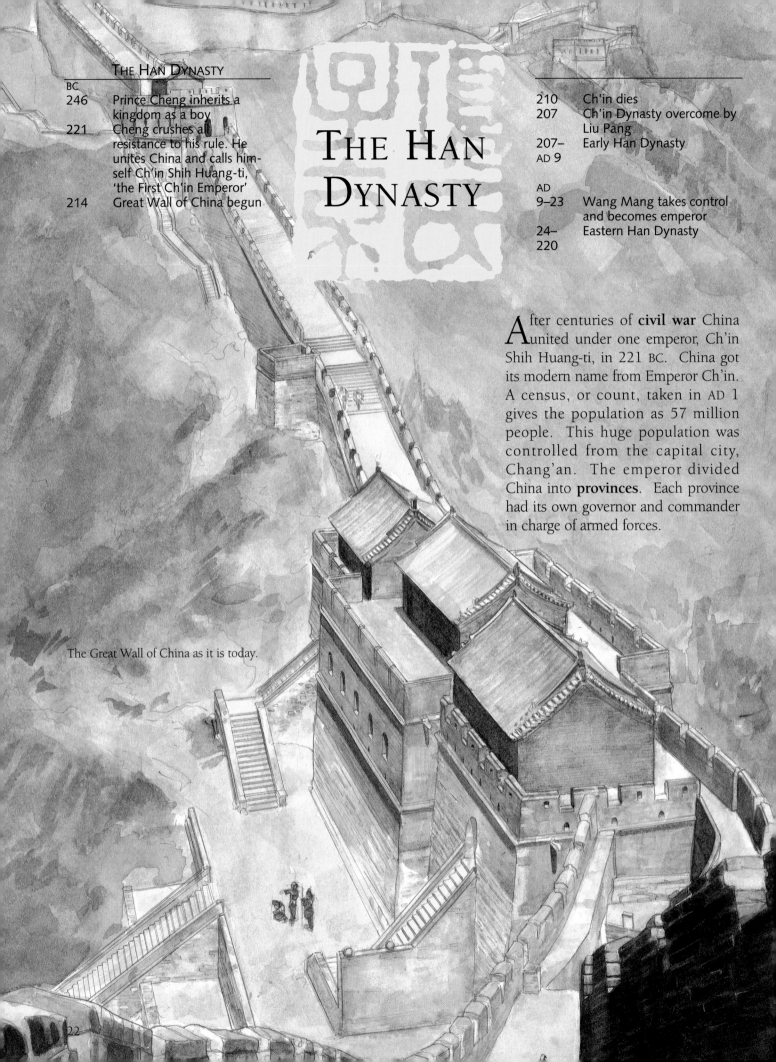

THE HAN DYNASTY

After centuries of **civil war** China united under one emperor, Ch'in Shih Huang-ti, in 221 BC. China got its modern name from Emperor Ch'in. A census, or count, taken in AD 1 gives the population as 57 million people. This huge population was controlled from the capital city, Chang'an. The emperor divided China into **provinces**. Each province had its own governor and commander in charge of armed forces.

The Great Wall of China as it is today.

BC	
250	All of Italy is controlled by the Romans
c. 185	Mauryan Empire in India in decline
30	Egypt becomes a province of Rome

THEIR LEGACIES

The greatest achievement of Emperor Ch'in was to create one country — China — after years of war. He was not liked by the people or the nobles because he was very ruthless. Ch'in standardised many aspects of Chinese life — laws, writing, money, weights and measures — which continued in use long after his death. The First Emperor is probably best known today for building the Great Wall.

AD	
29	Jesus Christ crucified
60	Kushan Empire established in India
79	Vesuvius erupts. Roman towns of Pompeii and Herculaneum destroyed
117	Roman Empire at its height
150	Rise of the city of Teotihuacán in the Valley of Mexico
224	Sassanid Dynasty established in Persia

SILK WEAVING

One of the most important goods the Chinese traded was silk. Silk is a **fibre** from the cocoon of the silkworm. Each cocoon produces about 900 metres of fibre threads. When the threads have been cleaned, unwound and then twisted back together again, the very fine silk is woven on looms like this one (right) into cloth.

EMPEROR CH'IN AND THE GREAT WALL

The full name of the Emperor Ch'in (above) meant 'the First Ch'in Emperor'. He established his own dynasty and died in 210 BC. But the system of government which Ch'in set up lasted in China until this century — in fact until 1912. Emperor Ch'in built a network of roads and canals across China and used his army to control any opposition to his rule. He also had to deal with threats of invasion from nomadic tribes to the north. Although there had been a series of earthen **fortifications** in northern China to keep these tribes out, Emperor Ch'in joined them together with a huge stone wall which became known as the Great Wall of China. It is the world's longest construction and stretches for about 2,300 kilometres. The wall is about 7.5 metres high and has watchtowers and defended gateways.

HAN METALWORK

There were many skilled metalworkers in the Han Empire. Beautiful objects were often made from bronze. This horse is only 34.5 centimetres tall and is said to be 'flying' because it has one hoof on the back of a swallow. It was one of many fine objects excavated from a tomb.

EMPEROR CH'IN'S TOMB

The painted wooden musician (above) was found in a Han Dynasty burial chamber.

Like many peoples in the world, the Chinese believed in life after death. They also believed that people would live the same sort of 'life' when they died. It was important, they thought, to take their possessions with them to the next life.

The tombs of the most important people in Chinese society were hidden deep under the ground and marked on the surface with great earth mounds. The tomb reconstructed below was 20 metres underground. We know from writings found with the body that it was the wife of the chief minister of the Kingdom of Changsha. To help preserve her body, it was wrapped in 20 layers of clothes and encased in four wooden coffins. Around the coffins were an enormous number of beautiful objects such as this lacquer tray (below), bowls, mugs and cups. There were fans, mirrors, clothes, boxes, little figures of her servants and food — chicken, sparrow, fish, rice and fruit.

The tomb was preserved with a layer of charcoal, and then a layer of solid white clay, which surrounded the wooden coffins.

THE TERRACOTTA ARMY

One of the most remarkable discoveries from the ancient world is the tomb of China's First Emperor, Ch'in. When Ch'in died he was buried under a huge mound of earth set inside a great courtyard. By the time of the First Emperor, servants were no longer sacrificed and buried with their masters and mistresses. Instead, thousands of life-size models of warriors were buried. You can see some of them in the photograph on the right. A Chinese historian tells us it took 700,000 forced labourers 36 years to build the tomb.

THE WORLD

BC

c. 200   Alexandria develops as the centre of Greek science and learning

c. 100   Celts develop defended settlements
Farming settlements in the south-west of America

THEIR ACHIEVEMENTS

*The tomb of the Emperor Ch'in was an incredible achievement. Each of the 7,000 pottery warriors, 3,000 footsoldiers, bowmen, spearmen and officers has a different face. There were also life-size pottery horses with their chariots. Some of the four burial pits of Emperor Ch'in's tomb were broken into long ago but in 1974 this pit (below), was discovered by accident, and found to be completely intact. It is being carefully **excavated** and preserved for people to see today.*

AD

14   Roman emperor Augustus dies

c. 100   Kingdom of Axum established in Ethiopia

c. 150   Rise of the city of Teotihuacán in the Valley of Mexico

224   Sassanid Dynasty established in Persia by Ardashir I

GLOSSARY

A

agents: people who conduct business on behalf of others. For example, a merchant might sell his goods to an agent, and then the agent will sell the goods to another merchant, who will in turn sell them to his or her customers.

archaeologist: someone who studies the past by scientifically examining the remains of the past. Archaeologists often **excavate** objects in their search for knowledge.

B

bust: a portrait (usually sculpted) of a person's head and shoulders.

Byzantine: the name that was given to the remains of the **Roman Empire** in the East after the fall of the last emperor in Rome in 476 AD. The Byzantine Empire continued until its capital, Constantinople, was raided in 1453.

C

caravans: the name given to groups of merchants in Asia and Africa who travel together across deserts with their goods carried by camels.

civil servants: people who run the civil service. Many countries have a civil service. The civil service is the organization that runs the government of a country.

civil war: a war within a country between different groups of people of the same nationality.

D

dammed: when a barrier is built across a river, the river has been dammed.

decipher: to work out what something means.

E

Edo: a member of the Negro people of Benin in south-west Nigeria. These people are well-known for their sixteenth-century bronze sculptures.

enlightenment: to have seen the light or the truth about life. This term usually describes a part of the prayer and philosophy of Buddhism.

excavate: to find and dig up an item from the past. Bones, objects, and entire buildings have been excavated.

exploit: to take advantage of someone for your own gain.

export: to sell and transport goods from one country to another.

F

fertile: lands that are capable of growing many crops or people who are capable of having many children are fertile.

fibre: a very thin thread of material or plant which can be spun or twisted with other fibres to make cloth, rope or a structure.

fortifications: walls, watchtowers, ditches or moats which defend houses, castles, towns or cities.

H

hectare: the name given to an area of 10,000 square metres.

hieroglyphic: a type of writing where symbols or pictures represent words, objects or sounds.

I

immigrants: people who have come to live in a country different from their place of birth.

import: to buy and transport goods produced in another country.

inscriptions: words, pictures or symbols carved into rock, bone, stone or wood.

irrigation: to water farm land by a system of small canals or ditches which carry water to the fields from a source such as a river.

Islamic: anything to do with the religion of Islam.

Islam was founded in 622 AD by the prophet Muhammad in Arabia. The followers of Islam are called **Muslims**. The holy book of Islam is the *Qur'an*.

J

jade: a semiprecious stone used in jewellery-making. Jade can be white or green in colour.

K

Kushan Empire: an empire in northern India which ranged from the mouth of the River Indus to the Caspian Sea and was established in c. AD 60.

L

lacquer: a hard, black or transparent, glossy coating made from resins found in certain trees.

Latin: the language of ancient Rome and the Roman Empire. Latin was used as the language of learning in medieval Europe. Books such as the Old and New *Testaments* of the *Bible* were written in Latin.

M

meditating: the process of thinking very deeply about a subject, usually a religious one.

Mesopotamia: an area of southwest Asia found between the Tigris and Euphrates rivers. This land was the site of many important ancient civilizations, such as Sumeria, Babylon and Persia.

millet: a grain crop grown to feed animals such as cows.

Ming Dynasty: a dynasty is a ruling family. The Ming Dynasty ruled China from 1368 to 1644 AD. The pottery and ceramics produced during the Ming Dynasty is thought of as being some of the finest in the world.

Muslims: Muslims are followers of the religion of **Islam**. Muslims are supposed to pray five times a day, give food to the poor, make a journey to Mecca at least once in their lives and abstain from eating during the hours of daylight while the religious festival of Ramadan is celebrated. Ramadan takes place in the ninth month of the Muslim year and lasts for 30 days.

N

Near East: the geographical area that includes the Black Sea, Persia, Sinai, Assyria and **Mesopotamia**.

nomadic: people who travel from place to place in search of food for themselves and their cattle.

O

oases: **fertile** places in deserts where water can be found.

P

palm oil: oil taken from palm trees and used in cooking.

Pliny: (c. AD 23–790) a Roman scientist and historian who also wrote about geography and the natural world.

province: the name for an area of land that belongs to a larger country or empire.

R

relics: something that has survived — usually something that has survived that is connected to a religion.

reservoirs: constructed lakes that are built to ensure a steady water supply for people. Reservoirs are usually made by **damming** a river.

ritual: a series of actions usually associated with a religious ceremony.

Roman Empire: the name of the lands ruled by the ancient Romans. At the height of Roman power the empire stretched from west and southern Europe to Africa and southwest Asia.

S

sacred: an object or building that is dedicated to one particular God, an object or place that is thought of as holy because of its connection with a religion or a god.

Sassanian Empire: this empire stretched over parts of India and the Near East around the Persian Gulf. The Sassanians took over the Parthian Empire in the third century AD.

Shona: the name of the language and the people of modern-day Zimbabwe and Mozambique.

Sogdian: people of central Asia who lived in the kingdom of Sogdiana. Their capital was Samarkand.

subcontinent: a large identifiable area of land within a continent.

T

Tang Dynasty: a dynasty is a ruling family. The Tang Dynasty ruled China from 618–907 AD.

tributaries: a body of water, such as a stream or a river that joins up with a larger river.

Y

Yoruba: people from west Africa, mainly from western Nigeria. The Yoruba lived in city-states and made beautiful art and music.

INDEX